To: _____

... for Making A Difference

From: _____

Dedication

I dedicate this book to all the children of the world who teach us exactly what we need to know about how to make our communities a better place to live, work and grow.

To my husband Craig for his willingness to grow in compassion with me. There is nothing more important in this life than those who are closest to us. Their love, happiness and time together is what makes a difference.

I'd like to dedicate this book to our children, for giving me a reason to keep going forward when times past were challenging and jam-packed full of opportunity to learn compassion for myself and then give it to others.

Mary Robinson Reynolds

MAKE A DIFFERENCE...

with the Power of

Connection

MARY ROBINSON REYNOLDS

HEART PRODUCTIONS & PUBLISHING

Copyright @ 2009 by Mary Robinson Reynolds
ISBN: 978-0-9628496-8-8
Printed & bound in the United States of America
Cover & text design: Heather Kibbey, Northwest Publishers Consortium

Heart Productions & Publishing
PO Box 56 · Newton Junction, NH 03859
Phone: 603-382-8848
www.MakeADifference.com

Table of Contents

The Connection That Makes A Difference 6

Make A Difference...with Compassion 12

Compassion: The Universal Language 22

Give Away What You Want 27

Make A Difference with Relabeling 34

The Power of Attention 42

The Helicopter Parent or Teacher 58

Fill Their Cups 71

It's All About The Connection 82

About The Author 92

The connection that...

Makes A Difference

*W*e are here to make a difference. It's what re-charges our emotional batteries. Reaching out to make a connection says: You matter to me, and I believe in you. Choosing to be affirmative is a powerful and profound way to positively influence today's children.

This gift book is a "think this" then "do that" and you'll "make it better" kind of a book. In the following pages I share specific, fundamental principles that really do work to make educating and raising children a rewarding, life-fulfilling experience. The rich content and touching stories illustrate how to turn even the most severe and unsettling situations with children of all ages completely around by how you connect.

Connection goes straight to the heart of the matter. This book gives you concise, instructive ways you can immediately begin "thinking differently" to positively affect children and be the difference you want to make. Loving and understanding connection, even in small doses, has tremendous power to heal a life.

Full Circle

My entrepreneurial trek, which has included work with adults and children in educational, corporate and personal settings, began over twenty years ago when I started to realize I knew something about at-risk youth that a large percentage of the educators I worked with would want to learn and would be able to easily incorporate into their daily classroom structure.

My special gift was that I knew, intuitively, how to heal behaviorally challenging children. My ability to create for them a sense of community and "belonging" helped them achieve measurably high levels of success, no matter how overcrowded my classrooms were.

I realized early in my teaching career that I had mentally done away with the "bell curve" and the "labels" put on behaviorally and academically challenged children by other well-meaning teachers before me.

When, as a sixth-grade teacher, I collected data from previous years of Stanford Achievement Tests, I found that the children arriving in my classroom each year were, on average, a year or two behind their expected grade level.

With my determination and guidance, through engaging instruction and the elimination of labels, they not only gained back what they had previously lost, but they achieved an additional two to three years of academic growth on their test scores.

In 1988, when I understood the effectiveness of my techniques, I began writing continuing educational programs to assist educators in learning how to heal all of the students in their classrooms who were living unhappy lives and not succeeding academically or otherwise.

The results of these programs were even more amazing than I could have predicted—teachers now had the tools they needed to deal compassionately and effectively with all children's learning styles and behavioral needs.

Then life happened! Legislation was passed that cut all funding for school programs such as mine.

The results were even more amazing!

I found myself redirected—led—into the corporate arena, where I quickly realized that we are all just little kids in big bodies! The principles and strategies I had been teaching educators, about breaking cycles of failure, worked in very diverse business environments, as well as day-to-day life. When parents learned how to heal themselves through the principles I taught them, their children thrived, and my teaching had a positive effect on adults and their children alike.

Connecting with compassion creates a ripple effect.

Now, nearly two decades later, I have spoken to tens of thousands of people, about the power of labeling and attitudes in communication. I've written six books, and started writing motivational poetry again for the first time since I was 18. My poems have become flash online movies and are available for anyone to watch at no charge and to pass along to others who would appreciate them. You'll find them at www.MakeADifference.com/movies

And this brings us to 2006, when I was sent a musical rendition of the Teddy Stallard story – a story, autobiographical in nature – written by Elizabeth Silance Ballard in 1974 about a little boy who almost fell through the cracks of the school system. I knew in a heartbeat that it needed to be a flash movie.

A year later, I received another true story about a Blue Ribbon Ceremony ™ created by Helice "Sparky" Bridges that literally saved the life of a 14-year-old boy. As I found myself now creating these flash movies, I realized that I had come full circle.

What I have found in the span of my personal and professional life is that connecting with compassion creates a ripple effect that changes attitudes, reinforces the positive, and can have an impact far greater than we realize. It is a simple act that leaves an imprint upon those to whom the affirmative attention is given.

At times our light goes out...

and is rekindled by a spark from another person.
Each of us has cause to think with deep gratitude
of those who have lighted the flame within us.

- Albert Schweitzer

Make A Difference with...
The Power of Compassion

Compassion turns "me" into "we." The moment that the "we" in "me" occurs, new understanding is revealed. In the midst of compassion we are able to instantly lay down our old habits of disapproval and judgment, and become highly discerning about what's really trying to happen for the greatest good.

Compassion is an old idea made new, because science has caught up to ancient literature and philosophy to prove that "the only way out" of resentment, anger, harmful or unskilled behavior is through compassion.

It makes you protective rather than controlling and when this occurs, you simply stop using fear and shame to modify unskillful behaviors. This one mental shift is what will dramatically and positively change unproductive behavior in an instant!

Compassion

It's about more than kindness; its about the essence and the power that compassion offers all humanity.

You will notice in this book that I don't talk about *love*. Love is ever unfolding and will ultimately be demonstrated through how you show up for the children in your care. I've worked with professionals, as well as parents, who, in their upset, say they just don't think they can love or help certain children.

Igniting Compassion

My response is simple: begin with compassion. I understand fully how challenging it is to feel love toward a child who walks through the door with the "difficult" factor. Compassion moves you right past what's difficult and on to matters of the heart. When you make an effort to see through the glazed-over look in these children's eyes, straight into their hearts, you will find your way. It's the affirmative connection that begins healing the negative beliefs these children embody.

I'm writing this book because, as a teacher who later became a counselor, I learned to keep it simple and straightforward.

I listened until I was able to learn some important basic information:

1. How the child was labeled at birth through his or her first five years of life, including both parent labels and school-related labels.

2. When working with parents, what was going on in the parent's life that the child could be carrying a symptom for.

3. If working with a teacher, what emotional buttons this child pushed for the teacher—necessary to determine how to best align the teacher with the child.

If I didn't readily see what needed to happen, I kept listening until I did. Wait for it. You must learn to resist the urge to analyze and fix too fast. When a problem seems so big that you don't even know where to begin, wait for it. Lean into the knowledge that this book provides.

Compassion offers a message that is universal. It is unifying, because it transcends the need to use force to counter unacceptable behavior that arises in disturbing circumstances and situations which an individual feels are beyond his or her own control.

We've all thought from time to time, "I just wish so and so would learn to be caring—or 'generous' or 'accommodating'—to others, and be more connecting and compassionate."

Its message is universal.

This is where we are presented with opportunities.

We somehow expect people who have no frame of reference to figure it out and "get with the program." It is not until we investigate a situation that we will be able to understand the reasons for unproductive behavior. Only then are we able to tap into the power of compassion, to change the life of a child.

And therein lies the rub. This is where we are presented with opportunities. Everyone can see that it's all about how "they" are behaving unskillfully. We tell ourselves that we have nothing to do with how horrible they are. They can't be changed. They will never get it. And yet, adults and children both are deeply affected and, yes, even changed by a simple act of compassion.

Connecting compassionately is all about how a simple shift in perception can bring new energy to any troubling situation. It's not about telling already stressed-out administrators, educators, or parents that they should be trying even harder with a child who is struggling. Trying harder, in and of itself, sends an attitudinal message to the child that says, "Because you are so hopeless, I have to try so hard to get you to get it!" This sets up a shame-and-fear cycle which compounds an existing problematic situation.

Force, shame, coercion, labeling and expulsion never did work—and never *will* work to create long term, life-enhancing solutions.

When you add compassion to any equation, consistently and repeatedly, it will bring immediate dramatic improvements.

When you are upset with a child, or an adult, for something disagreeable or harmful they just did, simply ask yourself: "Which is more powerful: anger or compassion?" Then ask: "Is what I'm about to say or do going to make it hard or easy to get what is for the greatest good out of this situation?"

To modify any unwanted behavior, we must remember in those most difficult moments that it's not about coming "at" problematic situations, nor is it about avoiding them. It's all about the emotional transformation that compassion offers.

Which is more powerful: anger or compassion?

To transform the emotions of an unwanted situation with any child or adult, you must first decide that you are—from this day forward—going to manage your impulse to abandon, avoid, diminish or punish to make your point.

Compassion never means being "walked on" and it never means "giving in" or tolerating harmful behavior.

What compassion afforded me, both as an educator working with challenging children and as a parent of three intelligent, strong-willed children, is that I never needed to use fear-based, hurtful, or shaming methods to get them to behave or do as I asked.

We all soak up compassion like a sponge when it's given to us. For me, compassion is what changes my reactions when I'm at the fork in the road, choosing compassion or judgment.

Compassion...
forms the necessary healing connection.

It's the moment that makes the difference. It's not flag-waving, march on, over-efforting that changes things. It's when something done in the moment, out of compassion, is remembered for all time. It's fleeting. It's there, and then it's not. And the only time you remember it is when you need it.

To people who say, "It's easier said than done," I say: "It's easier when done!" When I first started out in education I was essentially—as most educators are—a rule-follower. But in my first year as a "rural school" teacher in grades 3, 4, 5 and 6, I quickly saw that you had to throw out all of the traditional teaching "sit still and be quiet" rules, because nothing would get done.

Then I married a football coach and, every three to four years, we moved from school to school to advance our careers. To make a difference, we accepted positions at a transient school, a very long way from anywhere. Three years later, this career path brought us the jobs of our dreams, working in the largest school in the state. As a result of my many moves, I've been in every kind of situation—violent and otherwise—that schools faced then and now. I found that rarely does a difference get made by rigidly adhering to a bunch of constrictive, fear-based rules. Making a difference is all about diving in and simply doing the thing that's in front of us to do.

The gift in compassion is that it frees us from attachment to an outcome. When we are free, we are already making a difference by what we then model and are compelled to do for others.

Access and embrace humanness...

To experience the power of compassion, we access and embrace humanness, both our own and that of others. I know you've heard the saying, "Walk a mile in my shoes..." Well, the second you put yourself in someone else's shoes, you begin to connect to the heart of the matter, and therein lies innate compassion. By choosing to feel our own vulnerability, we can then accommodate the vulnerability of another.

By putting compassion first, you actually regulate the reactions that historically have triggered upsetting emotional responses. You can re-wire your impulses. The next time you become aware that you are emotionally triggered by someone's unskillful behavior, immediately visualize a crying child.

Bring a lost, lonely child to mind. If the image of a lost child or the little child in this photo instantly connects you to your heart, then commit it to memory. If neither of these images does it for you, then find a "heart-connecting" visual that will. You can manage yourself in the heat of any intense moment by shifting your focus to a broken-hearted child. It doesn't matter whether the child you see is a boy or a girl. Whichever connects you to your heart is the one you will use to regulate yourself. When you focus upon a mental image of a child in pain, you will find that no matter how upset you were a moment ago about whatever happened…now, it just doesn't have any impact. You'll find yourself literally laying it down, as you embrace the heart of the matter.

Our purpose in life is to make a difference. Compassion doesn't solve problems. It gets you into the best frame of mind and heart to reach beyond where you've gone before. It allows you to find new, creative, peaceful and healing solutions. Kindness is nice, but compassion gets the job done!

Compassion is...

the capacity for feeling what it is like
to live inside somebody else's skin.
It is the knowledge that there can never really be
any peace and joy for me
until there is peace and joy finally for you too.

– Frederick Buechner

Compassion—

For most people, the problem with being compassionate is that we fear if we offer it, we'll somehow be condoning and encouraging hurtful behavior. Yet, as we connect with compassion, life can be changed for the better, with changes lasting the span of a lifetime.

The real power of compassion is choosing it in the midst of difficult situations involving behaviors that we find upsetting and entirely off-putting. How can one be expected to be compassionate in the midst of unacceptable behavior?

The Universal Language of Mankind

How indeed? And yet this is what the stories in this book are all about. This *is* what's possible. From the letters I've received since I launched the *Make A Difference* movies, I know that examples of profound compassion happen all the time, with people like you and me. If you've received this book as a gift, it's probably because you are making a difference in people's lives all the time. Have you stopped to think about the wonderful changes you're initiating?

Wouldn't it be nice if it happened even more often? That's why I'm writing. Because it is you and I, the people who read books like this, who need to reach for the power of compassion even more than we already do.

We all make a difference. The question is: what kind of difference do we make?

When we see children or adults around us behaving unskillfully or inappropriately, with actions that are intended to affront or cause harm, they need our understanding and compassion.

This is the fork in the road, where we find we have a choice of either compassion...or judgment. It's important to understand that compassion does not mean that you condone hurtful or unskilled behavior. Instead, it's reaching into yourself to relate to people with a heartfelt energy of compassion that they can hear and assimilate.

Everything that irritates us about others can lead us to an understanding of ourselves.

— Carl Gustav Jung

Every time I've chosen compassion, I find I am deeply astounded, not only at the power of this force, but that it really works to shift and change a situation.

We often miss an essential point. When you go to that compassionate place that's deep within yourself, to look at the person who is doing something upsetting, you are not only giving compassion, but you are also receiving what you've just given.

You simply cannot launch a negative attitude or a judgment at someone and still feel peaceful and good about yourself. During those moments, it's impossible to feel lovable or safe.

There has been a significant amount of research about compassion, in the areas of human development and behavior.

Psychologists have demonstrated that a compassionate response to difficult people and situations yields a positive reaction 70% of the time. Whereas, responding with resentment or anger produces a negative reaction 100% of the time!

So which odds would you choose?

Compassion: Positive Result 70% of the Time
Resentment: Failure Result 100% of the Time

As I've illustrated in my book, *Attitude Alignment: The Art of Getting What You Want,* if you want the problematic situations in your life to dissipate and improve, start "throwing compassion" at the person or at the problem behavior. I know it sounds too simple, but try it. The next time you are upset, throw compassion at the problem and see how the situation changes before your very eyes.

The stories in the following pages of this book are small but powerful reminders of what the highest and best part of you already knows: that compassion makes us protective rather than controlling. The difference is crucial in creating long-term, life-enhancing results.

To get what you want, you must give away what you want.

My first experience of putting this principle into practice was when I was thirty-something and had just transferred to a school whose guidance counselor had to take an extended leave. A third-grader named Jamie Lynne was on my individual counseling schedule and her teacher described her as very angry and highly volatile.

Give Away What You Want

Jamie Lynne was pointed out to me in the lunchroom my first day, and what I observed hurt my heart. She was sitting at the end of the table with her little friend Anne, when five other girls approached them. By their demeanor, it was apparent that these five girls considered themselves the elite of the class. They sat down at the table and began taunting Jamie Lynne. Anne tried to stick up for her friend, but the girls continued their harassment.

Jamie Lynne became verbally volatile and the girls made fun of her. A teacher on lunch duty came storming in from across the room and started chastising Jamie Lynne for disruptive behavior and for yelling obscenities at the five "innocent" girls.

I moved in quickly and lightly touched the teacher's shoulder and asked if it was all right with her if I addressed the taunting behaviors of the five. She stepped back, and I proceeded to let the five girls know that I had seen everything they had said and done to Jamie Lynne. But Jamie Lynne was not able to hear my defense of her.

Since she was so used to taking the fall for other people's attacks, she didn't stop to hear that I'd just stood up for her. Instead, she jumped up and ran off with her tray, refusing to stay and hear what I had to say to the other girls.

I did not feel the need to control Jamie Lynne's behavior at this point. It was painfully obvious that she was on her own when it came to dealing with her classmates. The teacher who had come up to discipline Jamie Lynne quickly saw what was really going on and shifted her attitude.

My first meeting regarding Jamie Lynne was with her teacher and mother. Both related only negative accounts about her increasingly volatile behaviors. She had been a sweet and wonderful little girl who suddenly turned angry and hateful in first grade. Nothing happened, of course, that could have caused this turn in her behavior according to the mother. Her conclusion, in her exact words, was that Jamie Lynne was just a "good seed gone bad," and she was learning to reconcile herself to this fact.

I knew I wanted control.

I sat and listened, but elected not to say anything to try to turn their thinking around at this first meeting. I knew, being the new counselor in this school, that I did not have any credibility built up yet, and I needed to have success with Jamie Lynne first.

Later that day, when I met Jamie Lynne coming down the stairs, I said, "Hello Jamie Lynne, I just visited with your mother today, and I'm really looking forward to having you visit with me soon."

Jamie Lynne took one look at me and screamed, "I hate you! I hate you and I don't want to come see you. You will never be as good as our real counselor. I hate you. I hate you. Leave me alone; don't you come near me. I hate you." And with that, off she went, as angry and as hostile as she could be.

My thoughts assailed me. My first thought was: "Oh my gosh, I hope nobody saw her speak to me that way. My credibility will be destroyed before I've even begun." My second thought: "Wow, how am I ever going to reach this kid?" Then my third thought: "Give away what you want." My fourth thought asked: "But what do I want?"

But how could I give it away?

And finally, it came to me. My fifth thought was: "I want control. How do I give that away?" I went back to my office, shaking. I sat there and pondered this most profound experience. I realized that first I needed to let go of what someone else might think of a child being so disrespectful of me.

29

I did that quickly. I knew the name of the game I was in. I was modeling a new way of treating all children, and with any new approach comes adversity and making the most of an opportunity. But where did I go from here?

"Give away what you want. I want control. Now, how do I give that away?" I sat quietly at my desk, mulling over these thoughts, and then I put myself in Jamie Lynne's shoes. My gosh, what a painful place for a third grader to live! In her shoes, I realized that the message she'd been getting from the adults in her life was that she was a "bad" girl that needed to be "fixed."

I decided to try a new tactic with Jamie Lynne. I would not position myself as someone who was going to fix her. So with that in mind, I wrote her a note:

Dear Jamie Lynne,

I like you and I don't want to change anything about you.

I would like for us to become friends. If you would like that, I would too.

I just want you to know that if you ever want to come and see me, I'll be here in my office.

Your friend, if you want,
Ms. Mary

As I headed out my door to find Jamie Lynne, she saw me coming and jetted into the girls' restroom. I followed her in. I looked under the stalls and there were no feet on the floor. She was hiding from me! I reached for the door that I thought she was behind and gently pulled it open. She reacted as if I were going to hit her. I quietly handed her the note then gently closed the door and left.

The next morning, she was at my door with her demands. She would come, but only with her friend Anne, and all they were going to do with me was play games. That was it!

I said, "Deal. When do you want to start coming?"

With each little success, she became eager to learn more.

Jamie Lynne and Anne came once or twice a week. She was initially very resistant and distrustful of any connection with me. Through the board games we all played, conversations gently unfolded and she became connected to me as someone who cared about who she was and how she felt.

Eventually she began trying some of my "techniques" for dealing with her classmates, and with each little success she had, she became eager to learn more.

The day I transferred out of the school to another position, she opened her arms to me for the first time, and gave me a big, long hug. I told her how much I loved her and knew she was going to keep doing a great job managing her feelings.

When you give away what you want...
you connect with what's needed.

I fought back my own tears as she cried and said good-bye. In giving away the need for control, control is no longer what's needed to remedy problematic behaviors.

This little story is a small but powerful reminder of what the highest and best part of you already knows: that compassion makes us protective rather than controlling. The difference is crucial in creating long-term, life-enhancing results.

Jamie Lynne's full story is included in my book:
*No Labels, No Limits: Healing Today's Children –
Lessons from a TurnAround Specialist*

To get what you want, you must give away what you want.

Give It Away

If you want love, give it away.

If you want respect, give it away.

If you want honesty, give it away.

If you want cooperation, give it away.

If you want compassion, give it away.

If you want control, give it away!

It's really very simple when you think about it.

Mary Robinson Reynolds

Make A Difference with...
Relabeling

"We all know that good teachers make a positive difference each day. Sometimes we just need to be reminded through success stories."

- Doris Voitier, Superintendent, St. Bernard Parish Schools
and recipient of the *JFK Profile in Courage Award*

*W*hatever we focus on—put our attention on—expands.

The power of connection is played out through how we label a child, and then is transmitted directly to the child through our attitudes. When we get in touch with our own attitudes, beliefs and resistance about any challenging situation we may be dealing with, we, ourselves, will be transformed.

And when we are personally transformed, we set new energy in motion that will instantaneously affect the lives of those children in our care.

All children come with kindness and compassion built right in. Our job is not to instill it, but to nurture it and watch it as it grows and blossoms.

You may be wondering how a compassionate act could possibly work with children who appear to be born bullies. Here is a true story about a serious situation involving a hard-to-manage first grader. Through compassion and a conscious choice to understand what was really going on, I discovered his innate goodness, while completely eliminating the need for punishing consequences.

Chip was in first grade when I arrived at his school as counselor. As with any new person on staff, I was brought up to speed on the students I'd be working with, the most troubled children in the school. The words that both the teachers and the social workers used to describe Chip were heartbreaking: they labeled him a bully, abusive, angry, uncontrollable and evil. It was shocking to me that they felt it was perfectly acceptable to label any child "evil"—let alone a first grader. How could this little boy, after being in school only two years, have warranted such criticism and disdain?

When they said "evil," I knew immediately that it was all about a child who lived with such great pain and hatred of himself that he felt the need to strike out and to hurt others.

Over the next several months, in my support group for boys, I came to know Chip well enough to know that he was neither evil nor uncontrollable. Then, one day, he threw a chair at his teacher. Since the principal was out of the building at the time, Chip was sent to my office. I knew that he had never previously acted with this much violence.

I sat down on a small chair which put me at his eye level, and I asked him what had hurt him so much that made him decide to throw a chair at his teacher. He replied that his teacher hated him and always had. He felt there was no way to ever get her to like him. So I asked him if he would tell his teacher this, with my help. He agreed, and we called her into my office.

As we talked to the teacher, still seated in the small chair next to Chip, I supported him in expressing his feelings. His teacher responded to his accusation with heartfelt compassion.

A child who lived with such great pain and hatred of himself...

She said that she didn't hate him and, in fact, she actually cared very much about him.

It was clear to both Chip and me that she really meant it. I also knew from having talked with her on other occasions that Chip's behavior really scared her, so she was often responding out of fear, rather than from the compassionate connection she was now offering him.

Then I asked Chip why he felt that she hated him, and he replied that he knew he was a very, very bad boy, and he didn't think anyone could ever like him. I was impressed by his ability to articulate his deep-seated belief about himself.

Still sitting on the little chair, I put my left arm on his shoulders. Then I put my other hand on his heart and started affirming what a wonderful, delightful, lovable child I saw him to be.

I explained to him the truth about himself. I told him that it was not about being bad at all, just that he sometimes tried to hurt other people because he hurt so much himself.

Chip's behavior scared his teacher and she responded out of fear.

I complimented him on just how well I saw him doing in group, and how I saw him taking some risks as he was learning to express his hurt feelings. I affirmed that I knew he would be able to express how he was feeling even better and better as time went on. I told him that being able to say how he felt instead of throwing things would make it easy to be friends with the other kids and his teachers.

I wanted to instill in Chip new, positive thoughts about himself. So I continued to affirm over and over what a wonderful, sweet boy I considered him to be, as I kept touching his heart.

I pointed out how special and brave he was for the work he did with me in learning how to express his hurt feelings.

I told him how proud I was of him for all the efforts I saw him making on the playground and in class, and that more and more children were liking him. I affirmed my belief in his ability to ask for what he needed.

As I was speaking to him, I gradually felt the weight of his entire body coming to rest on my right hand next to his heart. It was a moment in time unlike anything I had experienced before. Like a dry sponge, he was drinking the affirmations into his entire being.

Up to this point, his teacher had feared having him in her classroom because she believed he was an evil boy. Chip's emotional interpretation of her labeling and her fear of him left him confused, powerless and hurting. It's natural for children to strike back when they feel they have been hurt. An adult must take the responsibility to help shed light on what has been causing the hurt in the child's life. Any aggressive act warrants immediate investigation.

What's the best that could happen?

When I was finished speaking, Chip's teacher gave him a big warm hug, told him she loved him and took him back to class. It is my belief that this approach allowed Chip to actually *become* "a good boy with some hurt that just needed to be worked out." Compassion and relabeling had everything to do with the dramatic improvement in his behavior which, I'm pleased to say, followed this incident through the remainder of the school year.

We are a society that labels, so why not select labels that will heal and advance a child's life experience. Certainly schools will continue to label children to identify additional needs. You can accept the diagnosis while intending a preferred prognosis. Labels define our attitudes. You simply cannot have an attitude and keep it a secret. We radiate our thoughts, and others feel this and respond to it. Children by far are the most susceptible to adverse labeling. A child's mind is a clear, sensitive palette that receives impressions without protection. Until children are fourteen years of age, their psyches absorb the suggestions and impressions of the predominant adults in their lives.

In my book, *No Labels, No Limits*—available at MakeADifference.com— I've written about five children who excelled because I relabeled them. Real life stories will give you more confidence in your own ability to accomplish relabeling for yourself. A new label doesn't have to be true yet, in order for you to plant the seed. Instead of talking about what you don't want, shift gears and simply describe in detail what you'd prefer to see happen with this situation. It's as easy to label someone *hopeless* as it is to label them *capable* in their own special way.

Think about it. What's the best that could happen?

Make A Difference with the Power of...
Attention

The greatest gift you can give another is the purity of your attention.

- Richard Moss

The real power of compassionate attention is that it causes positive behavioral change—instantaneously.

Connection is about more than simple acknowledgment; it's about the necessity of reaching out daily to be emotionally available, through compassionate attention, to the individuals in our lives, no matter what age.

You can make a difference in how well children do, both at home and in the classroom, by the kind of attention you decide to give them.

When you remain consistent in offering attention in a positive and behavior-affirming way, it becomes a "conscious" act that offers profound healing to a child. This, coupled with a decision to simply slow down and energetically connect with individuals, will create alignment that generates long-term solutions.

How you decide to give your attention will determine how easy it will be to enjoy and get along with children on through their adolescent years.

"Behavior-affirming attention" includes our true attitude behind the tone in our voice, the language we use to teach or to offer choices, and the age-appropriate expectations we put in place for children.

Before you can change anyone else...

You'll find that the very best place to begin is with *Behavior Modification's #1 Rule*: Before you can change anyone else you must first change yourself.

You simply cannot have an attitude and keep it a secret! If you don't like a child, you will not be able to work with that child successfully. You are either contaminating or contributing to an outcome based on what you've decided about any given situation.

To see an improvement that's immediate, you must change your attitude: fear, judgments, entitlement, prejudices and condescending labels. Do this, and you'll affect and heal unproductive behaviors, seeing better results than you could have imagined.

44

Change your attitude, and you shift the resistant energy between you and the child in an instant.

you must first change yourself.

To learn how you can directly affect a child's energy, please watch my Energy Illustration video training: MakeADifference.com/attitude

Children sense if you attitudinally see them as the enemy and their behaviors as bad, bad, bad. Children know if you don't like them or see them as an energy drain, a nuisance and a bother. As adults, we know this too. The only difference is that we've learned over the years how to pretend we don't feel what we feel, know what we know,

or want what we really want. Children learn from us how to become the label that has been put on them.

You must give positive regard to children if you are to receive respect. We teach people how to treat us. It is incongruous to expect children to be respectful when you are not respectful in your attitude and your treatment of them. It's like pushing a child to the ground, putting your foot on her shoulder and yelling "Get Up!"

Children's IQs are already highly developed by age two, so if you engage children of all ages in two-way communication, they can learn to "use their words" to discuss, rather than "act out," what they are feeling and needing to communicate.

You teach children how to be accountable for their behavior by simply asking them to share what's going on with them that is causing them to do what they are doing. Asking "what" not "why" raises their emotional intelligence, and will eliminate habitual excuse-making. Once the thinking and the feelings are voiced and understood, the two of you can come up with an agreeable solution.

Age Appropriate Expectations

The number one mistake many professionals and parents make is treating children as if they should know better! Why would they know better?

When dealing with a situation, ask yourself this question: "Is this behavior normal and age appropriate?" Then ask: "Has this child previously been taught how to deal with situations like this?"

Children are open books. You tell them that if they do this, they can expect that, and they believe you!

When you label a child, or think of him as a "problem" child, he believes you and will experience problems.

Children are open books. If you tell them they can expect this, they believe you!

If you tell a child that he can prove himself to you and earn your trust, and here's how, he believes you and will want the benefits your trust will give him as he earns it.

New York University research studies have proven that the expectations of the teachers were carried out in a profound way.

The children in the study were given an achievement test, and the students, who had a wide range of scores on the tests, were randomly assigned to two teachers. One teacher was informed that all her students had the highest scores on the test, the other was told his students had the lowest scores on the test. Even though the students were randomly assigned, they actually performed according to the teachers' expectations.

The teacher who thought she had all the high scoring students had them performing at high levels of achievement, while the teacher who thought the students in his class were the ones with low test scores, found that his students performed poorly in his class.

They began to see that their thoughts and expectations did make a difference.

After revealing this information to the teachers, they began to see that their thoughts and expectations did make a difference. If we think Johnny is going to be a loser, or that Suzy is going to flake out, or some child is incapable of concentrating on his work, it's going to be exactly as predicted. Why? Because our thoughts and feelings carry tremendous "energy in motion," and our beliefs cause us to act in accordance with the expected outcome. Children are strongly affected by the energy of your expectations.

A Stanford University study showed measurable and dramatic acceleration in reading speed and comprehension when they renamed the Remedial Reading Room to Accelerated Reading Room for the school year.

To let children and adolescents know that you believe in them and expect their very (age appropriate) best, tell them repeatedly, using affirmative language, what's great about them. Tell them that you believe in them. Communicate your expectations clearly and slowly, then ask the child to repeat them back to you.

Teach them ways to replace undesirable behavior and to manage their pain, fear and frustrations. Role-playing in private for just a few minutes gives them the skill they need to feel and do better.

In dealing with chronic behaviors, minimize both your attention to them and the importance of these unproductive behaviors. Make a conscious decision to increase your attention and give acknowledgment for preferred behaviors as they are occurring, until the new behavior becomes the norm. Then simply and consistently attend and acknowledge.

Teach them ways to replace undesirable behavior.

In one of my teleconference trainings, the principal of an elementary school discussed the case of a first-grade boy who had been behaving badly for several months, biting other children in the hallway, seemingly at random. Nothing they had tried had eliminated this behavior. I asked if she had observed how the other children were treating him—attitudinally and verbally—as they passed him in the hallways.

There was so much attention on the severity of the boy's behavior that the adults had overlooked the clues. When she decided to stand out in the hallway, to watch what was really going on, she discovered that the children being bitten were the actual offenders. This boy was just fighting back, the only way he knew how.

To resolve a situation like this, it's necessary to work with each of the children involved, to answer this question: "What's going on inside you that makes you treat someone this way?" Then, together, role-play new ways to deal with the hurtful or offensive behaviors of others.

Attention Deficit Disorder

Food and environmental allergies can directly affect a child's mood, as well as his ability to focus and have normal amounts of energy. However, a little understood fact about children engaged in excessive attention-seeking behavior is that they truly are deficient in attention. That is why ignoring them never heals the underlying problem causing their behavior.

How often have we heard ourselves say about a behavioral problem, "that child just needs attention," as if to say needing attention is bad, not relevant or important. The child is displaying a symptom of something going on in his home and/or school environment.

In covering the topic of the "power of attention" in one of my corporate trainings, a woman told me that her sister was in the hospital dying of kidney disease. Even when faced with her sister's life-threatening illness, the woman and her family continued to say, "She's just doing this for attention!" Her sister had been diagnosed with ADHD— Attention Deficit Hyperactive Disorder—and had displayed "pay attention to me" behaviors since childhood.

She was terribly concerned now because I had just covered the importance of being willing to fill someone's cup with the simple act of time and attention. What I had just presented made her realize that never once had she or her family considered the validity of a person's need to feel love and connection through attention. I told her the greatest gift she could give her sister now was simply connecting with time and attention. In the month that followed, before her sister died, the woman was finally able to understand the value of this gift.

Research conducted as far back as World War II revealed the power of touch and loving attention to abandoned babies. Psychological and physical stunting of infants deprived of physical contact, although otherwise fed and cared for, was noted in the pioneering work of psychoanalysts John Bowlby and Renee Spitz, who observed children orphaned in the war.

Recognizing the validity of a person's need...

New research suggests that the lack of certain brain chemicals that are released by touch, attention and connection may account for an infant's failure to thrive. And yet, many in our society still wrestle with an internal debate about the relevance of simply filling our children's "need for attention cups" with the loving attention that every human being does, in fact, require for survival.

There is probably nothing more challenging for any adult—educator or parent—than feeling the pressing demands of day-to-day life and work, while faced with a child or children needing an appropriate dose of time and attention.

We have children failing to thrive not just because of their home environments, but also because their need is so great that the educators and helping professionals feel overwhelmed at how to begin to fill so many empty cups.

Without positive expectation and attention, children coming into our schools who are not being fed emotionally at home will have difficulty maintaining behaviors that are conducive to learning.

to feel love and connection through attention.

Many of the attention problems children experience today arise from the harsh messages they receive. Among these is the still-existent, ever-pervasive authoritarian model—that if you give children too much positive, affirmative attention, you will spoil them and teach them to be self-absorbed, even arrogant and narcissistic. The exact opposite is true.

Children teach us exactly what we need to know.

Although research has proven conclusively that it is the "lack of positive regard, affirmative attention, rules, and unconditional love" that can, and will, instill all those unwanted, self-absorbed behaviors, we still think withholding love and attention will somehow correct undesired behavior.

What about children whose singular emotional connection comes from receiving everything they want in the form of material things? I think you already know the answer to that. Material things will never fill an empty cup. So you might as well roll up your sleeves, put the credit cards away, and learn to attend and listen with new, healing ears.

How much attention is too much, and how do we know when it's not enough? We can know immediately through the behaviors a child is displaying.

Children teach us exactly what we need to know. Behaviors speak. It's just that we, through our experiences, have learned to be forceful, fearful or shaming about dealing with undesirable behaviors.

To make a real difference in the lives of struggling children, we must learn how to be non-resistant to displays of attention-getting behavior by learning more about what the behavior is trying to tell us. The more resistance we have toward undesirable behavior, the more the behavior will be magnified.

The message is clear: When a deficit in connection is not met with emotionally positive attention, unhappy behaviors will burst through children in ways that bring attention, one way or another. We've over-analyzed something that's quite simple.

For example, when a child is being referred to as "manipulative," what is actually happening is that we have a child who is not getting her needs met. The child has simply learned, from the adults in her life, how to get her needs met—either negatively or positively—through some form of manipulation. Yet, we label the child as a "manipulator," as if this were a "bad" thing. Instead, this behavior merely offers information about what the adult is teaching the child she must do to get attention.

I once worked with a family that came to me for counseling because they believed their four year old daughter was destroying their marriage. Their exact words to me in our first session were, "From the minute she was born, she's been controlling and manipulating us." They said that she had been colicky when she was only a week old. Their own parents—the child's grandparents—had warned them that she was manipulating them!"

The power of the grandparent's label upon this infant had charted her behavioral path.

Behaviors speak...
and we must learn to listen.

Together, we examined age-appropriate behaviors for infants through age four. We re-labeled her as their "sweet, sweet girl," and by the second counseling session, she was responding quickly to her new labels and enjoying normal behaviors and play.

I've seen far too many permanent file records on children with this behavioral description. This is where professionals and parents must search for understanding, to be careful not to let this kind of labeling take root in their thinking.

Children know they are loved and cared for by the adults in their lives who attend, touch, teach, coach and give directives with clear expectations and positive regard. Children also know when they have, inadvertently, become the "enemy." They feel this from how they are being treated.

How fast can things go wrong? Very fast. Children or adolescents can interpret their parents' lack of connection and attention—their lack of time or personal acknowledgment—as an indication that they are a bother and a nuisance. They experience this as a lack of love, and depression and thoughts of suicide can set in.

Expression of love through positive attention, touch and togetherness is the only way to ensure that children will thrive. These fundamentals are necessary for developing self-esteem. Self-esteem comes from a cup that is consistently and appropriately being filled with regard, acknowledgment and positive expectation.

When we resist, resent, dismiss or ignore filling a child's cup, because we are afraid of threatening behavior, or are pre-occupied, too busy, or functioning immaturely in our own adult lives—or if we believe that attention spoils a child—we are ignoring the clear signals and making a situation increasingly problematic.

When the American Pediatric Association conducted research with children ages three to eighteen, they found that the top two complaints children have about the significant adults in their lives were these: "not listening" and "yelling."

Which brings up an interesting point: children who have only known this kind of negative attention from adults become addicted to negative behaviors so they can feel a connection.

Another interesting point is that yelling is experienced not only in volume but also as attitudinal energy. You can speak to a child in a quiet voice, but if you are attitudinally condescending or angry, they will hear and feel what you are saying as yelling. After all, you can't have an attitude and keep it a secret!

If you really want to make an immediate difference in a child with behavioral and/or academic challenges, simply be willing to sit with yourself and answer the following three questions:

- What is the truth about how I really feel about this child?
- What can I do attitudinally to make this situation better?
- How do I prefer that my experience with this child be?

Connection...

ensures that

children will thrive.

The Helicopter Parent or Teacher

Excessive attention—hovering—is equally destructive and unhealthy for a child's psychological and emotional development and will guarantee one of two outcomes.

A child who is strong-willed, or has neurological personality wiring that is overt, is more likely to resist and become extremely defiant. A child with a more covert, thoughtful or passive neurological personality may take on a "victim" or "I can't" behavior.

Excessive attention, repeating directives and constantly checking-in is a put down. It teaches your child to be self-absorbed, instilling the "it's all about me" world view. Through constant helicopter hovering, trying to know every detail of your child's life, you are basically saying, "You are incapable of managing your life without me."

Invasive attention is irritating to a child's psyche and energetic physiological system. Visualize children growing into competent and capable individuals, and that will benefit them more.

"Hovering like a helicopter" with persistent, pointless and repetitive "Make sure you do this, remember to do that," aggravates the emotional and psychological health of any child. It will create negative reactions, and lower the child's self esteem and ability to navigate their world with growing confidence and maturity.

Mr. Rogers speaks of Limits...

Call them rules or call them limits,
    good ones, I believe, have this in common:

they serve reasonable purposes;
    they are practical and within a child's capability;
      they are consistent;
and they are an expression of loving concern.

-Fred Rogers

"Inside" Voice

When my son was little, every night at bedtime, I would lie down on the bed with him to read. If there had been a problem that day, this would be the time he would access his feelings and want to talk about it. Largely because of my counseling background, I knew the value of just listening and not fixing.

Rather than *tell* him what he should do, I simply said, "Let's both get really quiet and listen to what our *inside* voice tells us would make this better." A few minutes later, he would tell me what his *inside* voice had told him to do to make the situation better. Invariably, what he "heard" was what I "heard" as well.

I knew that the only way my children would ever be safe in the world as they grew up was for them to learn to listen and trust the quiet *inside* voice, known to most as intuition. But, you say, "What if my children hear a different voice from what I would tell them to do?" Then you simply listen to the child's reasoning in order to determine if it is, in fact, the *inside* voice or *outside* voices of society and fear. Intuition, after all, never causes harm to oneself or others.

When my son was eleven, he was headed up the hill on his bicycle to his friend's house. I told him that because it would be dark soon, I did not want him coming down our hill fast. He was to take it slowly.

I taught him to listen to his "inside" voice.

After dark, I caught him speeding down the hill and barely making the turn into our yard. When I asked him what was going on for him—that he would not do as I had specifically directed him to do—he said, "My inside voice told me to go fast."

Was that his intuition or just an excuse? Of course it's fun to ride down the hill at top speed, but he did that every day, so he understood that this was a special request. I knew he would be coming home after dark and I just felt it would be safer.

Knowing my son, I think he got scared in the dark and felt the need to get home as quickly as he could. Inside voice or fear? Possibly both. Because I was teaching him the importance of listening to his inside voice, I supported his interpretation and didn't feel it would "teach him a lesson" to take his bicycle privileges away. It paid off in more ways than I can list in this book. All three of our children are world travelers and have the ability to slow themselves down and wait for inner directions and answers.

This is the one thing that gives me ease as a parent when I think of my grown children traveling on the highways and byways of their lives.

Consequences!

An educator and parent's number one job is to foster self-esteem by encouraging age-appropriate dependence while allowing autonomy to develop. Interdependence

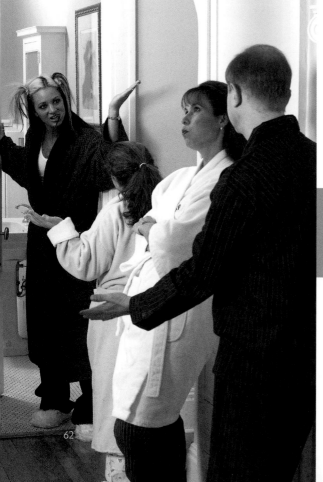

is a most healthy emotional state which is learned through two-way communication. Most communication between adults and children is one-way, and that's why it fails to bring about desired behavior. If you are having a very difficult time with teen-agers, it's because you have an attitude, and you are not genuinely extending positive regard or offering a respectful connection.

Expect a rollercoaster ride?

If you subscribe to the belief that life is going to be a rollercoaster ride when children become teenagers, then that belief is "your attitude," and you are most definitely programming an expectation that will become a self-fulfilling experience.

If your attitude is anything but compassionate positive regard, it is interfering with any attempt to communicate. You must modify your attitude by re-labeling your limited beliefs about what your experience will be with teenagers. Start connecting with compassion. It's not easy for teen-agers to be with adults who consistently launch their negative, limiting "attitudes" at them.

Deborah Yurgelun-Todd is the director of neuropsychology and cognitive neuroimaging at McLean Hospital in Belmont, MA. Her recent work suggests that teens' brains actually work differently than adults' when processing emotional information from external stimuli. In a recent study of mapping differences between brains of adults and teens, Todd put teenage and adult volunteers into an MRI and monitored how their brains responded to a series of pictures. The results were surprising. When she examined their brain scans, Todd found that the teenagers were using a different part of their brain when viewing the images.

Then that's exactly what you'll be getting!

There was an age-dependent or age-related change between the ages of eleven and seventeen, with the most dramatic difference being in the early teen years. One aspect of the scientists' work has been to look at the frontal part of the brain, which has been known to underlie thought, anticipation, planning and goal-directed behavior. They studied the relationship of this part to the more inferior, or lower part, of the brain, which has been associated with gut responses.

The frontal lobe, the executive region that was studied, is not always functioning fully in teenagers. That would suggest that teenagers aren't thinking through the consequences of their behaviors. Now this explains so much!

Onc of the implications of this work is that, in relationship to emotional information, the teenager's brain may be responding more with gut reaction—impulsive behavior—than with an executive or measured, thoughtful response.

Realize that, if teenagers are not fully developed in thinking through consequences of their behavior, then younger children certainly are not either.

Shaming children into behaving does not teach them to use their judgment, but rather teaches them that they are incompetent, incapable, irresponsible and inept.

This actually induces more of the unwanted behavior, because we are coming "at" the unwanted behaviors instead of using the language of positive reinforcement, expectation, directives and choices.

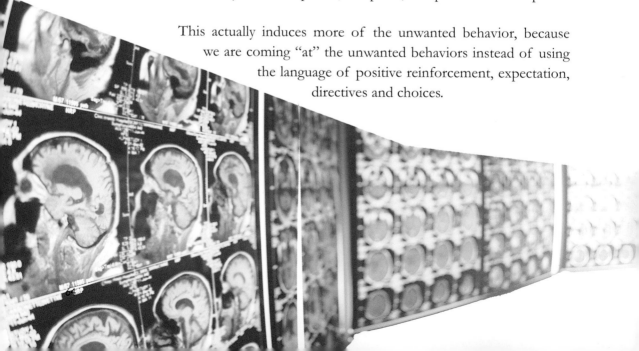

Frontal lobe development research now helps us understand how a compassionate response—activating the frontal lobe—to an emotionally upsetting situation soothes problematic behaviors quickly.

This also explains why making desired behavior about the "consequences," rather than teaching choice-making and skill acquisition, does not teach them a lesson!

Repeatedly threatening harsh consequences will never instill the skill acquisition you want to see children and teenagers growing into.

To read more about Deborah Yurgelun-Todd's research findings, go to:
www.MakeADifference.com/teenbrain

The teenage brain responds more with gut reaction than with a measured, thoughtful response.

So what do you do with children or teenagers who are out of control, causing harm to themselves or others? Do this:

- Give ongoing acknowledgment, positive regard and behavior-affirming attention.
- Make a connection—use two-way communication about behavioral expectations.
- Offer choices, stating best case scenario preferences. Ask the child what he "thinks."
- Role-play when needed to empower and teach a new skill. Ask the child what she "prefers."
- Re-label. Suspend your fear and judgment.
- Teach them in very clear terms how they can prove themselves to grow more trust.

By age five, a child hears "No" over 40,000 times.

Research indicates that, by the time a child is five years old, he hears the word "No" over 40,000 times and "Yes" only 5,000 times. Certainly there are times when the answer must be unequivocally "No," but as the adult, I've found those times to be the exceptions not the rule. With our own children, we used the following two phrases to eliminate overusing the word "No."

Two magical phrases to the rescue!

Instead of saying, "No," try these two magical phrases:

- "I understand that…" and
- "*n-e-v-e-r-t-h-e-l-e-s-s*"

Be in an Attitude Free Zone when you say: "I understand and accept that you really want to take off with your friends and go to the mall; *n-e-v-e-r-t-h-e-l-e-s-s*, this time you will not be able to, because I need your help with errands."

When the child balks and says, "But all of my friends are going," you repeat yourself: "I understand how much you really want to be with your friends; *n-e-v-e-r-t-h-e-l-e-s-s*, this time I need you to stay on deck and help me out with our errands. There will be a next time. I'll even drive everybody, and a good time will be had by all."

Regarding children wanting to buy things, in our family we validated every single thing that our children wanted to buy. When they wanted to buy unexpected things, we would say, "I agree; that would be a really cool thing to buy. However, at this time I have not budgeted it in. Let's put it on your visualization board and see what happens."

When they were old enough, we gave them allowances, so they could save for whatever they wanted. They could visualize and budget ahead with our full support, as they were learning how to manage their desires and money.

It's not age appropriate for children between the ages of three and eighteen to be accomplished in the areas of trust and responsibility, without appropriate levels of skill acquisition, checking-in, support and encouragement.

Connecting with compassion...

Having the experience with teaching and counseling thousands of other people's children before having my own definitely gave me the tools I needed to raise healthy, happy children. But I will admit that when it came to my own children, it was emotionally much more intense. I know what it feels like to want to helicopter! But I had seen the results of children being deprived of touch, attention and connection as well as the children who had been over-attended. So I worked at making time to connect, touch, love, but not over-attend when faced with the parental grip of fear for "my poor baby!"

More times than I care to remember, it would have been quickest just to say, "Sit down and be quiet" to my children, when we needed to get somewhere and were already late. I also never used physical force or spanking to instill appropriate behaviors.

Spanking, as well as verbal shaming, is simply an adult temper tantrum. Physical, verbal or attitudinal abuse neither trains nor educates. These tactics are simply the angry outbursts of adults who are not making the time to learn new ways to heal generational legacies of pain and abuse.

We raised three strong-willed, highly-intelligent children—in a blended family—and never once did we utilize hurtful or harmful control methods. Causing harm to another never works to achieve a desired outcome.

is effective with all ages.

Yes, our children made age-appropriate errors in judgment, and never once did we throw the "there will be painful and harsh consequences" tactic at them.

And, I never once sent any child to "the office" from my classroom or counseling session. I never once abandoned or rejected any child in my care. There is no need to when you simply slow down, get quiet and connect with what's really going on.

If you are a parent having a problem with your child's teacher, or you are a teacher having a problem with a child's parent, this same "connecting with compassion" approach will not only work with children of all ages, it will work with adults as well.

Certainly, our society has work to do to change this legacy of pain. We see children in our schools and on our streets struggling to get the touch and attention they need, either through unproductive behaviors that bring attention or through their escape into drugs, alcohol, sex, food, shopping and involvement in cliques or gangs.

While our children were growing up, we were building our business. Because we had a blended family, I also made it a point to make sure my husband's daughters felt welcome, wanted, loved and enjoyed every time they came in the door. I was truly happy to see them when they arrived home from school.

There were definitely adjustments, attitudes and stress in our joined family. Yet the children always got to be heard, even if what they had to say was emotional. Everything was valid. Venting was allowed, and peaceful, loving solutions were always found. We consider ourselves truly blessed that our three children have enjoyable relationships with each other, have graduated from college and are leading healthy, productive lives.

Venting was allowed, and peaceful,
loving solutions were always found.

70

Filling The Cup

I've always been a sucker for attention.

- Cuba Gooding Jr.

In my work with educators as well as business professionals, one of the biggest concerns about time and effort is dealing with children or adults who are extremely "needy," and who suck the energy out of you day in and day out.

The reason why you feel a drain on your energy is your resistance to the need for attention.

There is a very easy solution: give it! Give needy individuals your undivided attention. Whether it's a small child, adolescent or an adult, the unwanted behavior will not cease until you fill that cup. Avoidance or trying to force or shame them out of their "neediness" will not create life-enhancing long-term results. So just fill their cup!

And here's how: you simply tell these individuals that they matter to you and that who they are really does make a difference. Tell them you'd like to make a pact with them that, from now on, you are going to be available for the time with you they need—with the following two guidelines:

First, if you are in a conversation with a group of people, on the phone or working with someone one-on-one, they must wait.

Second, they must be willing to ask you, "Is now a good time?" If it isn't, you explain to them exactly how many more minutes you need before you can sit down and be with them.

Here's what will happen: at first, they will need you often. They will test the guidelines you've put in place. When they do, you simply repeat your criteria with the expectation that they can wait. You may say something like, "I know you can wait X more minutes, right?"

If you really want that cup to get filled, while at the same time teaching them they can manage themselves, so that their need for "fill my completely empty cup" attention will level off to a normal range, then when you are with them, you really must be with them.

The longest it has ever taken me to fill a cup ...is just two weeks.

You must not watch the clock. If you have an upcoming appointment, let them know what time you must leave, and set your cell phone alarm to ring so you both know that it's time for you to go. Be fully present—emotionally available—with them. Listen with healing ears. Simply enjoy their uniqueness and idiosyncrasies, and this relatively small amount of time will, in fact, fill their cup. Productivity will increase, and you will have a healthy environment and meaningful connection.

Of all situations involving children or adults, where I've applied this cup-filling method, the longest it has taken for the cup to be filled was two weeks.

That's all the time it took for the person to be functioning with a new sense of autonomy. In most situations, the matter was resolved within a week. Remember always that what you resist, persists, and what you focus on, grows. Which brings me to a true story about a child who behaved like a wild monkey, causing hourly disruption in the classroom...

Treat a person as he is, and he will remain as he is.

Treat a person as if he were what he could be,

and he will become what he could and should be.

– Goethe

Filling Randy's Cup

When I walked into my seventh grade classroom on the very first day of that school year, I found Randy standing on top of his desk screaming and jumping around like a wild monkey! He was a highly intelligent boy, who had learned that by behaving wildly and out of control in front of his classmates, he would be able to fill his cup with attention. By the time he reached middle school he had already been labeled as SED (Severely Emotionally Disabled). I had been informed that Randy's own mother didn't want him, and he lived with his grandmother most of the time. Over the years, neither one of them had attended parent-teacher conferences. Randy was essentially on his own.

Mr. B., the Behavioral Specialist, had worked with Randy all through sixth grade. Each day Randy worked with Mr. B., he would come back to the classroom just as out of control as when he left. By the end of the first week of school, Mr. B. confided in me that he considered Randy a lost cause. The Specialist didn't believe there was anything that could be done for the boy.

When I heard Mr. B.'s "attitude" about Randy, I knew it would be unproductive to continue to send Randy to him for help. I told him that it was fine with me to try leaving Randy in the classroom. Great relief washed over Mr. B.'s face. However, I suggested that Mr. B. meet with Randy the following day, to give me an hour to visit with my class about my plan: "Operation Concentration."

Some teachers and parents believe you've got to have school-wide Positive Behavior Support in place before you can reach out and help a child.

To convince yourself that you have to wait until a school has, and reinforces, clear behavioral expectations, is to simply choose not to step up to the plate. Yet there's one philosophy that always works: "If it is to be, it is up to me."

When you are faced with a situation like this, understand that everyone is involved whether they wanted to be or not. Because I'd had success with all the extremely challenging students I'd worked with, I decided that the three hours I had with Randy in my classroom were going to be enough to fill his cup for a lifetime. I was going to see to it that this was Randy's best school year ever!

I decided to ignore the sarcastic, disparaging remarks from Randy's other teachers about his behavior. I sensed that if he got his cup filled every day in my classroom, it could play forward into his other classes.

The next morning, while Randy was with Mr. B., I opened a Community Meeting with the class, and explained the direction we would take as a compassionate community this year. I had a few guidelines that I expected them to follow firmly for two weeks.

I told them that during the first week of school, I'd noticed that they were participating in Randy's disruptive behavior, whether they realized it or not. I acknowledged that they might not like him, because he had a history of wild behavior in school and would often do aggravating things to them or their work.

Then I allowed a brief open discussion about their own personal feelings and fears about Randy, from previous experiences with him in earlier grades. With each example they gave me, I helped them to understand how they may have inadvertently "participated" with Randy in generating a negative experience. In helping them understand how their own "attitudes" about Randy stimulated more loud behavior, they began to understand how it must feel from Randy's perspective and how he reacted strongly to their attitudes. At the conclusion of our community meeting, I shared with them my three expectations for *Operation Concentration* for the next two weeks.

Operation Concentration

1. No Throwing An Attitude, no Eye Rolling, no Egging Randy On—or you'll hear from me about what Attitude Adjustment you need to make.

2. You have the right to look to me to intervene immediately when Randy, or anyone else, is invading your space and keeping you from your work.

3. Your job is to remain neutral and to concentrate on your work, without rolling your eyes or "throwing an attitude" at Randy. You have my permission to say, "Randy, that's not okay, please stop it now." If Randy doesn't stop, I will intervene.

I explained that, as we became neutral about Randy's behavior, it might escalate. By not getting negative attention the old way, he might become louder and even more invasive. We role-played how launching attitudes does, in fact, escalate anyone's behavior, and they began to understand their part of the equation. We also role-played how to concentrate and give zero attitudinal energy toward Randy when he was acting wildly and trying to get their negative "attitudinal" attention.

When Randy arrived back from Mr. B.'s, I asked Mr. B. to sit with my class while I took Randy into his office to explain how things were going to proceed this school year.

I told him I wanted him in my classroom full time, and that I had asked Mr. B. to release him to stay in the classroom with all of us. I told him that in this year's class—our special community—his wild monkey behavior was no longer acceptable. I said that I had put some guidelines in place so that neither he, nor anyone else, would bring negative attention on themselves. I explained to him that I felt that his acting like a wild monkey was just his way of hurting himself, and I could not allow him to do that any more. I cared too much, and I wanted him in my classroom.

Telling "unwanted" children with huge abandonment issues that you "want" them in your classroom is a healing soothing balm for them. Repeating it often continues to fill their cup and that big gaping hole in their hearts. A healed heart and a filled-up cup solve all kinds of behavior issues.

I told him that I saw him to be a wonderful, talented, smart—maybe even genius— young man, and I expected him to have his best year ever with our class! I also framed it as "our" class, so he would begin to take ownership as a member of our community and class. All for one and one for all would be our motto!

Together, we returned to class where everyone was on Operation Concentration! Randy expected to get some attention as he walked in with me, but no one looked up. He went over to his desk, and tried to engage the student behind him. The child looked up, gave a kind smile then went back to work. Then he tried to aggravate the student in front, then the one to the side. I was watching him peripherally. Everyone stayed focused and neutral. As children came up to my desk to ask their questions, Randy began to escalate his behavior, leaving his desk and going over to some of the students who had historically taunted him. They all continued to concentrate, remaining neutral as they did their work. They looked at me and I looked at them. We had silent communication going. Everyone could feel the difference.

Randy went over to the book case, shaking it to throw the books on the floor. He looked to see who was watching. No one paid attention. Everyone kept working. Over the next hour, Randy tried in vain to get a rise.

I did an occasional, attentive walk-by, expressing positive acknowledgment to each student's work as I went. Randy, who was emotionally undone, had not joined his group or opened his text book. There was nothing I could praise him for, so I asked him if he'd like to come up to my desk and do some work together to get started on the assignment. It was just enough of an invitation to give him some relief. He asked if he could put his desk by my desk. I said that I'd love to have him up by my desk so we could get the assignment underway.

So back and forth he went—my desk, his desk, my desk, his desk—asking really meaningless questions, just needing to feel my proximity, my energetic connection and care. I greeted him each time with heartfelt interest and a readiness to listen to whatever it was he wanted to ask. He was officially "wanted."

In the next two weeks, Randy continued to be disruptive, as he attempted to get negative attention from his peers. He'd try to cause classroom havoc, to fill his cup the old way. But little by little, the members of the class who had previously hated and taunted him, began to acknowledge him accommodatingly, as they had observed me doing not only with Randy but with each of them, for their participation in creating the best classroom community this school had ever seen!

A healed heart and a filled-up cup solve all kinds of behavior issues.

The Ripple Effect

As time went on, I began to notice that, in the hallways on the way to his other classes, Randy held his own with the older kids who had upset and teased him over the years. I even saw him skipping along with joy from time to time, as he was headed to his next class. Reports came in that he was doing well on the playground and that he even had made a few new friends.

My focus was solely on what I could accomplish with the three hours a day I had with Randy, and the other students who needed their cups filled. A review of the previous year's achievement test results revealed that 50% of the children in this class were considered to be at-risk and failing, while 50% were in a moderate to high academic range—a huge number of children whose cups needed to be filled!

Because of Randy's history of extreme behavior, his classmates quickly embraced the hope and directives I offered consistently, from the very first week of a new school year, until we grew into the community we envisioned.

I did not concern myself with what might happen when he went to his other classes, or what might happen to him in his home environment (unless I suspected abuse, and then I would most certainly have intervened). I did not concern myself with what was out of my classroom unless I saw someone mistreating him in the halls or lunchroom. I trusted that his experiencing what it was like to feel "wanted" and to be an "insider" in our community would go a long way.

As the school year went on, I happened upon a conversation between several other teachers, talking about Randy in glowing terms, saying that they didn't know what had changed Randy, but that he was definitely doing so much better in their classes.

At the last parent-teacher conference of the year, his mother showed up, for the first time. I raved on about how wonderful Randy was, how intelligent and creative I found him to be, and what things I wanted him to continue to improve on. There was a quiet acknowledgment between the two of us, as I read pain coupled with relief on her face, that her child was happier and having a productive year.

"And the day came when the risk it took
to remain tight inside the bud
was more painful
than the risk it took to blossom."

-Anais Nin

Connection

It's All About The Connection...

Relationships that work do so because of how people are deciding to connect. It's never about that we can't connect. It's that we must be willing to put compassion first. Whether you are skeptical or hopeful, when you simply decide to think compassionate thoughts, the power of the feeling that is ignited is palpable. The connection to another is instantly available and deeply real.

Connecting with compassion disarms every imaginable type of difficulty. I'll never forget the time I was coming down a school hallway just as a fight between two 200-pound football linebackers was erupting. A crowd was forming and verbal expletives where flying everywhere. Pushing and shoving had started and fists were drawn just as I was arriving. Knowing that anger is all about perceived pain, fear and shame, I stepped right in between the two students, looked straight into the eyes and heart of the one doing the most hollering and firmly, yet compassionately, asked, "What do you think this guy has done to hurt you?"

Everything stopped. I could feel the crowd of onlookers take in a breath and hold it. The hallway was suddenly silent. The angry young man's eyes instantly welled up with tears and he yelled, "No matter how @%#*! hard I try, he is always mean to me and he just doesn't like me!" To which the other young man yelled back, "I like you! I just hate the @%#*! stuff you do!" The first young man, in a voice of shock and disbelief replied with a faint, "Oh."

There was a moment of silence as they both looked at each other rather dumbfoundedly. Then they both turned toward their open lockers and started fumbling with their books as if nothing had happened. Knowing that they needed a moment to collect themselves, I moved the crowd that had gathered along to their classrooms.

As an elementary and middle school teacher and as a high school guidance counselor, I can't tell you how many scary-looking bullies I've had the privilege to work with over the years. All it ever seemed to take, in the midst of their angry tirades was to connect from a compassionate place, and ask them who they thought had hurt them enough to make them feel this upset.

Every single time I did this, tears would burn their eyes almost before I could get the full question out. Their tears never ceased to amaze me and I'd fight back my own tears just so I could move them forward into their own personal understanding of the emotional build-up that had welled up within them. From there, we were able to work on the real problems surrounding the unacceptable behaviors that got them sent to my office in the first place.

Some people misinterpret what compassion really is. It's neither sympathy nor empathy. The goal here is not to feel sorry for a child, nor is it necessary to "identify" with him or her. What is powerful—and life-changing—is connecting with the child who, as an individual, is totally competent and capable of learning in the ways that, together, you find work best.

Compassion is neither sympathy nor empathy...

When you are able to surrender your need to punish, judge and label children out of fear and a belief that you must be strict, rigid or harsh to control them into behaving, you will be able to access compassionate attention more readily and easily.

Compassion is, after all, a deep awareness of the suffering of another, coupled with the wish to relieve it.

If what you are offering is compassion, you will feel a lift in your energy. That's the real power of it. There is absolutely no force to it, so there is no energy expended. Everyone feels better, not worse. The only "work" necessary is remembering to interrupt yourself—in the midst of old reactionary behaviors to certain types of people and situations—to make a conscious choice to put compassion first.

When you are compassionate with others, you feel it for yourself. When this happens, you feel a softening throughout your entire being—your psyche, your shoulders, your back…and your heart. If this happens for you, then you can also know it's happening for others.

Behavior-affirming attention is one thing anyone can give that has the potential to make a lasting difference. In working with children like Chip, Jamie Lynne and Randy, I did not attach the level of my giving to what they would or would not do.

It takes just three simple steps to create a classroom and/or home environment where individuals collectively will become self-managing and highly productive.

The Three Simple Steps...
to A Compassionate Environment

Step 1: Change your mind and you change your relationships. If you currently see certain children as "problem children," then you are not seeing the inherent greatness in them that's trying to get out. You are inadvertently making them feel like the enemy. When you allow yourself to be seduced by unskilled or hurtful behavior, you miss what they are teaching you. Children teach us exactly what we need to know…if we will just pay attention.

Slow down and take a few moments to look past the behavior, to see what's really going on. It takes less than a minute. The willingness to be open to a shift in your perception will instantly lift your own energy and will change things for the better as you now reach out to connect to the heart and genius within each child.

Step 2: Think Community. You must hold firm to the concept that your classroom or home environment is a safe haven. It's all about *community*, where every single child is included and is expected to show up and belong. When you witness one individual doing something verbally or attitudinally harmful to his peers or siblings, i.e., his community, you simply and quietly take the child aside and address what's really going on, openly and compassionately.

Think Community

At this pivotal moment, you only need to say one thing to individuals who have been hurtful: "What's going on for you that you would do (or say) what you just did to so and so?" If they don't know, simply say, "If you did know, what would it be?" If they still can't access what's actually upsetting them, then say, "When you do know, I want you to tell me. We will revisit this before the end of the day. For now, let's get back to work."

That's it. This very specific technique interrupts what's happening and transforms any unproductive experience with children, adolescents and adults.

It lets them know that, even though they've been unskillful in their treatment of others, they matter to you. They now have your full compassionate attention, and they know that you want to help them with whatever it is they feel they needed to strike out about.

Step 3: Repeat Steps 1 and 2 as often as needed for the next nine weeks. By then, you'll have a classroom or home environment that's a community where all individuals are included and are expected to show up and belong. They will excel beyond any predicted level, and you'll reap benefits for holding firmly to this goal.

There is a heart that beats within every single one of us. Connection calls the heart of the matter forth in ways that are beyond our human understanding. How compassion works is a mystery. With behavior-affirming attention, there is a whole range of positive possibilities.

Research about the brain reveals that compassionate thoughts literally light up the frontal lobe of a person's brain. (The frontal lobe is where the mind can access solutions.) When we are resentful or angry, there is no light in that part of the brain, and so we shut down and fail to function well. As soon as we deliberately think compassionate thoughts, this part of the brain lights up, and we can literally go from "impossible" to "possible" in an instant.

Compassion is, after all, a deep awareness of the suffering of another, coupled with the wish to relieve it. It is truly wanting others to be free from suffering. And when we offer this, we have made a difference.

There are times when we think our actions have not made a significant difference—and that can be disheartening. What's important here is to take heart in those moments.

Remember always that you receive the instant you give and, in that, you can trust you've made a difference in someone's life, because you felt it in your own.

You can trust you've made a difference in someone's life because you felt it in your own...

You just need ...

9 Weeks to a Make A Difference Year!

Why nine weeks?

Every school year, I felt that the first nine weeks of school set the stage for how the entire year would go. I knew—down to my toes—that if my student's social needs were all dealt with, they would be highly functional the rest of the school year, and classroom life would be good. In working with parents, I told them to be laser-focused on the things I wanted them to accomplish, with an end-goal of just nine weeks. It takes only nine! Any nine weeks will do. You begin when you begin.

Through teaching children, educators and parents how to create a compassionate community and/or home environment, we dramatically raised emotional intelligence.

How did I do this?

My goal was simple. I placed the children's emotional needs first—above my concern about making it through X number of pages a week. Raising their emotional IQ's dramatically improved their ability to focus and function academically. Every time an emotional situation played out in the classroom, lunchroom or playground, we had an open discussion, no matter how long it took that day. The key is to stop expelling, excluding or abandoning kids. Everybody in the environment is involved. Be compassionate, and everything gets better.

And now, I'm giving you my 9-Week School Curriculum, in support of education, which you'll find at: www.MakeADifference.com/curriculum

What's something that anybody can do?

Let people know that they matter. The I Make A Difference™ wristband is affirmative and will be absorbed by the psyche. It's a great way to acknowledge how important everyone within your sphere of influence is to you. It's also a peripheral reminder to each child, adolescent or adult receiving and wearing this wristband that we are here to be a living example of what humanity can be.

Self-esteem actually comes from getting outside ourselves long enough to experience what it means to be a part of something greater than ourselves. This is our purpose and passion. As we own that "I Make A Difference," we experience a full and ever-giving "cup" ...and this, after all, is what it's all about!

www.MakeADifference.com/wristband

♥ The 9-Week   School Curriculum ♥

Educational Psychology, Counseling & Development

Mary Robinson Reynolds, M.S., an educational psychologist, and master trainer, is the author of six books: *Make A Difference…with the Power of Connection, Make A Difference…with the Power of Compassion, Attitude Alignment: The Art of Getting What You Want!, No Labels No Limits, You Are A Success!, MasterMinding for a Rich Life, MasterMinding 101®* online course and *Stay Married* online course.

As a professional speaker, Mary's dynamic presentation range covers the spectrum from subtle, spiritual and endearing to outrageously, side-splittingly funny, to hammer-the-point intensity. She is also a wise and somewhat bawdy soul, masterful at helping others trust that what they desire is valid.

As an author, she writes as she speaks, with vocabulary that's familiar and funny. Her advice is direct, not airy-fairy encouragement, to get people going with the changes they know they need to make. She opens your "heart" with gentle, probing questions like, "So how do you really prefer it to be?" and "Why do you think you can't have it?"

There is nothing more important to Mary than her husband, children and extended family and friends. She feels she lives an amazingly rich life, having put her faith first, her family second and her passion for world healing and peace third. Her husband, Craig, was able to join her in the production of online flash movies and publishing business in 2004. She feels her greatest of all achievements is her blended family with her husband's two daughters and her son.

Life should NOT be a journey to the grave with the intention of arriving safely
in an attractive and well-preserved body, but rather to skid in sideways,
chocolate in one hand, wine in the other, body thoroughly used up,
totally worn out and screaming, "Woo-Hoo what a ride!"
Mavis Leyrer of Seattle, age 83

In acknowledgment of my editor and book designer, Heather Kibbey of Panoply Press, Lake Oswego, Oregon, (npcbooks.com)—woman extraordinare—as I call her, who thrilled me every day with her creative inspiration and genius for this book. I think you'll agree with me, that what she has done with this book is amazing, profound and has heartfelt beauty. One of the most enjoyable aspects for me as a writer is when I begin to see my words come to life in the book formatting process. Every day with Heather's incoming page designs is like opening present after present. With each new book I write, my gift receiving quotient is always abundantly filled!

I'd like to give a heartfelt thanks to my son, B. J. Robinson and my sister, Markreta Brandt, for their "last look" editing of my books.

It's important to me to acknowledge my amazing MasterMind partners for their ongoing support and help in achieving Make A Difference goals and dreams: Craig Reynolds, Judy Pearson and Kate Nowak, for without them life would be difficult, not to mention bland.

To my husband Craig: I must say he signed on for quite an adventure when he married me. Not only was I a mother of a young son, I was very ill at the time. I'd overextended myself in an effort to create a career as a professional speaker and author. Previous marriages brought their own stresses into this "let's make a difference" journey. Through the years of creating our business together, we got to learn how to connect more compassionately. We consider ourselves blessed to be able to build a rich life and marriage filled with enjoyment of each other and our truly wonderful children.

Photo Credits:
Photos for the Randy story on pages 77-80 are by Jani Bryson. Her work is available at: www.janibryson.com

Other photography: photos.com, istockphoto

Background image this page: citrusmoon.com

As a TurnAround Specialist and MasterMinding Maven®, Mary Robinson Reynolds founded Heart Productions and Publishing in 1990, to build on her success as an educator, coach, consultant, entrepreneur, speaker and author.

Heart Productions & Publishing creates and markets inspirational products that meet the needs of all people wanting to heal their lives in areas of relationships, time, health and money.

Since its inception, Mary's primary interest has been to lift and elevate people working on the matters of the heart. So our goal, like our name, is to heal people's minds and hearts and to renew their spirits.

If you have enjoyed this book and wish to learn more about our flash online movies and our full line of beautifully designed products and resources that really do make a difference, please visit us at:

www.MakeADifference.com

Millions of people throughout the world are being uplifted and inspired by Mary's movies. Compelling mind-body-spirit research concludes that music has the power to reduce stress, enhance cognitive functioning, and improve productivity and creativity. Music, combined with inspired messages of hope, restores faith, renews the mind and opens the way for peaceful solutions.

Mary is a woman with a big philanthropic heart. She has created a simple system to assist people and organizations who are making a difference. If you would like to use Mary's "word of mouse" movie and Gift Book in a campaign to expand the reach of your organization (exponentially) and to raise money, simply click on the Fundraising link at our website and read how we can help you help others.

For corporate gift-giving and incentive programs, please call:

800-639-8191

With Make A Difference ...with the Power of Connection, *you have already taken a step toward a greater humanity. Now take the next step and learn how to make a lasting difference in the life of a child.*

NO LABELS, NO LIMITS: HEALING TODAY'S CHILDREN
Lessons from a TurnAround Specialist
by Mary Robinson Reynolds

In her exciting new book, *No Labels, No Limits*, educator, psychologist and author Mary Robinson Reynolds, M.S., explains how a change in they way you "think" will instantaneously affect unwanted behavior and produce a preferred outcome. The creator of the *Make A Difference* movies offers real-life strategies and stories that illustrate the importance of adults in a child's life. Learn how a shift in your perception lets you make your own Magic with today's children.

Stories to inspire and heal include:
Melison: *The Family That Couldn't Do Math*
Brandon: *Wrong Side of the Tracks*
Chip: *When A Child Is Labeled "Evil"*
Crazy Josh: *The Biggest, Baddest Sixth Grade Class!*
Angry Jamie Lynne: *Give Away What You Want*

Children who are out of step with their peers, exhibiting learning or behavior problems, are fortunate if they meet a top TurnAround Specialist like Mary Robinson Reynolds.
Sadly, many teachers and parents have no access to professional help and so out-of-step kids routinely fall through the cracks of our educational system.

Now teachers and parents can learn the techniques for identifying underlying causes of unwanted behavior and eliminating them, helping these troubled youngsters find the path toward a happy, well-adjusted childhood. A great book for beginning to understand the energetic power of a label.

"A book every teacher and parent must read. It gave me such hope that I could make a difference in the lives of these children." - Vern Kennedy, Child Advocate

To learn more about this irresistible book please visit us at:
www.MakeADifference.com/children

TAKE THE NEXT STEPS WITH HEART PUBLISHING & PRODUCTION

Make A Difference Flash Online Movies are part of a series of inspirational movies created by Heart Productions & Publishing's Founder, Mary Robinson Reynolds.

For more resources and gift books, please visit us at:
www.MakeADifference.com

At our website you can join our free *Make A Difference Newsletter*, and watch our inspirational movies daily, to enjoy the benefits of a peaceful, renewed mind, body and spirit.

Popular gift items are available, such as meaningful Jewelry, motivational Posters, Screensavers, Downloadable Movies and DVDs, plus Online Courses, Interactive and Inspirational books.

You are welcome to send our free flash online movies to those you appreciate and care about:

www.MakeADifference.com/movies

Sit back, relax and let Mary's movies lift you up so you can make a difference in someone's life today!

info@MakeADifference.com
1-800-639-8191

**Make A Difference with the Power of Connection
...and we will see World Peace in Our Lifetime.**